MW00782112

EMERGENCE

KAMARI BRIGHT

7 Publishing

www.7-publishing.com

Los Angeles, California

ISBN-13: 978-0692718841 (Seven)
ISBN-10: 0692718842

Copyright © Kamari Bright

Book Cover Design By Austin Willis "Visuals By Willis"

Table of Contents

"Intro"

I write because there are certain things I can't say. It's

not for lack of words, but, more so because I was born a

listener. Although that's perfect for your average talker,

it often leaves me without anyone to talk to. It didn't take

many attempts to fit everything I felt into the forty second

attention span of your average talker, or many trivially

interrupted outcries before I just stopped trying. Have

you ever had someone interrupt you, mid-feeling and

mid-sentence, to blurt out some insignificant observation

about a stranger's headband? That shit hurts. To be in-

advertently told that what you have to say is less im-

1

portant than a hair accessory, or the mismatching of an outfit. Or a recently ordered drink that hasn't arrived in record time. Or the thoughtless postings on a social media site that will be there long beyond your moment of vulnerability. That hurts more than keeping things bottled up. So for a time, I thought that was the solution. Choose the lesser hurt. Keep things bottled up.

And I did. I held on to my hurts like a parasitic fetus in the womb. I made them more important than anything else. Validated them. Fed them bitter tears, anger, solitude. I helped them grow. They were no longer a little cluster of cells, but a full-grown infant that looked like me and everyone else that contributed to my hurts. But, naturally, pregnancies end in labor.

I didn't know what to do. I cried. And screamed. And lashed out. And just didn't know what to do. I had felt little cramps before, but nothing like this. This baby that I had nursed within me for years felt like it was killing me. I needed to get it out. There is no hurt that stays perfectly and neatly inside. It all surfaces somehow.

Many years ago, I gave birth to my first hurt and called it a poem. It looked like the dad who didn't care enough, the mom who cared too much, and the companion I never had. It looked like me. And the labor pains lessened with each new child. I bore a child for my sorrow. I bore a child for my angst. I bore a child for my uncertainties. Pregnancies became shorter and shorter.

Although they are my loves and carry so much of me in their seams, I realize I cannot hold them close forever. I have to let them find their place in the world; outside of me. My hope is that these children of my life experiences will induce your own into labor. That we will all release our hurts from ourselves. That we will not succumb to the trial of labor, but will make it through to proudly proclaim

"These are my offspring..."

BREATHE

"Courting"

I fell for myself

Cuz only I knew how to love me right

I liked myself

Took myself out

Held my hand

Kissed my lips

Missed myself when I left for too long

Couldn't contain myself from my self

Until

Myself got old

And I could predict my own habits

Because I knew better than anyone what to expect

From myself

So I distanced from myself

Lost interest in myself

Neglected myself

Cast myself away

Hurt myself better than anyone else could

Cuz only I knew how to love me, right?

"Reciprocity"

i tangoed with Karma through a series of interludes

golden ring of restriction on my feet

she followed my lead

while i fumbled through box steps

and walked through trots

she never told me the dance was wrong

never stopped me

until the snippets stopped and songs started to play

Ring Passed

she took lead

but now i wanted to dance

i knew the steps, feet unbound

no le importaba

i watched her reincarnate ill-created choreography

clinging to me

fumbling, stumbling

then when the song reached its peak

and she furiously danced her dance

she lost her balance

falling to the ground, grabbing me

as we fell, with a twisted smile on her face, she whis-

pered

something i never knew to understand

Karma

"HER"

On the road from Paradise to Insanity

I lost my queen

Lost my queen and walked the line looking for her

Lost her and no one could help

No search parties

No crown

Streets ran into each other

Destinations disappeared

I walked asleep in cold sunshine

Cast away glance of Horus

I lost HER

Lost her and no one else realized they lost her too

Our mother, wife, lifeline, love is gone

No return home without her

Disdain of the nation at my heels

Foreign grave in my view

Lost

"Request"

I thought it was jewelry

On the days I'd left home

Without my badges of femininity

I felt uncomfortably there

Like post-shame Eve

Although only Adam was in sight

Anyway

I thought earrings were my vanity

Until I drove myself blind to finally see a face

And when I saw it

My eyes couldn't bear

To remember what I'd forgotten lives ago

That it was my light

My light was my only redemption

It was my only vanity

I looked at you

In your state of undress

And became aware of my oldest fear

I've never asked much of anyone

But with earrings in hand

And humility in tow

I beg you

Never let them see me without my light

It is the only connection I have

It is my only piece of God

If there is nothing else you ever grant me

Don't let anyone see me

Without my immortality

"Graduation"

I left from safety in search of a storm

Traded blue and white skies for grey and darker grey

swirls

sirens signaled me to retreat

Frenzied men told me what was to come

I hummed "I'll never turn back no more"

I went to tornadoes in search of release

Left mundane boxed rooms for deadly uncertainty

Cars oppositely passed me

Raced home to straw-made securities

I sang "no more, no more"

Queue the lightningthunderhailrain

Let the sky fall from its place

I looked my reflection in the mirror

And believed her when she sang

"No more, no more, no more my Lord. I'll never turn

back no more"

The tornado never came

Though the winds did blow

Leaving remnants of leaves chaos and turn-backs-no-

more

And I never turned back, and I won't turn back, no I'll

never turn back

no more, no more

"Vibration"

I have reached a moment in my life where I am vibrating.
Not the part of me that is firm and measurable, but the
part that drives everything else. It's a terrifyingly excit-
ing thing. Exciting in that I can make things around me
move from my own movement, and terrifying because I
am unstable.

Combustible.

So I touch things to watch them animate. I watch and I
move. Because if I stop I'll see that there is no peace in
this vibration stage. No calm for something that has no
still.

Right now I'll put everything around me in motion and
maybe forget my own.

"Retrieval"

There are some things that you have that I'd like to get
back

I was in a rush when I left because I knew you wouldn't
come after me

This isn't a movie

I was in a hurry because I had to get away from that fact

And amid the fleeing I forgot a bunch of things at your
place

Please don't think I'm being vindictive, taking back eve-
rything I ever gave

It's not like that

You're a good person

That never changed

But we weren't good

That's all

And normally I'd just say 'forget it, I can buy new things'

but I couldn't live with the embarrassment if I didn't get

them back

Knowing that one day someone would be visiting you

And see the laughter I left in the corner of your living

room

The thoughts hanging on the rack in your bathroom

Or the embraces that were heaped on the floor on your

side of the bed...

And they'd ask 'what's this?'

And you'd say 'just some stuff somebody left'...

Just like that

I wouldn't have a name

Barely a reminiscence

An X

I'd be a letter when I used to be paragraphs to you

And honestly I'd be embarrassed

So please

When you get a chance

Give me back my things

While they've still got their color

Please don't let them dust over like they were never sa-

cred

Please...

"Ride"

Blurred lights

Like highway shooting stars

Hypnotizing

Beautiful then gone

Listening to him tell me about a girl who went wrong

But I knew her

Probably better than he did

Nobody can tell you about a girl gone wrong better than

the wrong girl

And that's where I came in

In a seedy establishment I sat stage left

Waiting for it

Waiting for my soul to join me again

And he he and he played

Plucked plucked bows and strings

Untied and wild

Kicked kicked tatted

Evasive elaborate composites

Taut and strong

Air bent wave rendered

Distorted and beautiful

Soft and beautiful

Wrath and beautiful

He he and he created

While I shed my skin and suspended in air

 On a crescendo

And I was there, I was free

And when it ended so did I

Disappeared

Snapped back to now

On this highway away

Headed to no-way

Pouring memories out the window like the ashes of a

moment I clung to

Too fiercely

"Seattle"

There are mornings when I wake up

Tuck my knees to my chest

Widen my dried lids to keep them from the solace of

each other

And I try to remember what it feels like

I search through the notches on my blank wall

The creased veins of my comforter

The yellow light breaking life into my soft black tomb

It's never there

So I lay still and close my eyes again

Hoping I'd etched the feeling there

On the back of my lids

Where other's eyes used to haunt me

And think maybe if I went deep enough into myself

I could find the memory

Maybe if I was immortal enough I could make a brand

new remembrance

But in my humanity I fall asleep again

And wake up rushed

Not toward the feeling I need to get back

But for the bus I need to catch

"Suite"

From my view on the penthouse floor of this hotel

I watch the sun set on its path

And I wonder if it will ever feel…easier than this

If hopes ever meet actions

And actions ever meet goals

And all the while all I really hope for is to see you smile

See you unhurt and light and so free that you'll float

In midair

And that'll be why people stare at you

Not because you absorb most of the rays of the sun

But because you are a ray of the sun

That's why I stare out the window of this penthouse

floor

Because I'm watching you, suspended over everything

that is beneath you

And I'd traverse this never-ending sphere

If it meant I'd never see you fall down

But they tell me not all hopes meet actions

Not all actions meet goals

And even those in the penthouse

Come tumbling to the ground floors

Yet here we are

BREATHE

"Memories"

I had us

In the palm of my hand

Could've been a memory

Or a photo

But we were there

Sitting on the porch steps of your granny's old house

In black and white

Doing nothing perfectly together

Probably synching breaths, or brain waves, or heartbeats

It may have been a picture

I can't remember

I only see us

At that house on that porch, motionless

Before the complication of color

"Pick-Up Lines"

I'm not attracted to you

but I see you as artwork

I could paint you right now if you wouldn't get offended

Starting with that richer-than-the-first-soil

deep brown skin that makes me wonder

how any flame that ever touched it could extinguish

and if my own mahogany ever grazed it

would I catch fire

That hue would be the first part I paint

No outline or confinements

It'd probably dominate my whole page

Even though you're not physically my type

I wish I could translate the way

That the gum you chew yields

for the sole purpose of giving movement to your lips

As they dance with a right of ownership upon your face

Purposeful and proud

And oooo I swear I'm not hitting on you

But

Let me document

The smoothness of your skin

Like peeled mango I would lightly palm your descrip-

tions

And know that if I squeezed them too tight

they'd slip right through my fingers

No I'm not tryna make you mine

But I'd take all the beauty of you

and lawfully wed it in print

By the power vested in my pen

I'd immortalize you in prose

Past sickness and health

Past time do us part

"Mona"

We humans are creatures of habit, you see

We adapt to situations for survival

Protection

Sanity

And when we find a mode of self-preservation that

works, we cling to it

That's the 'habit' part there

Like this smile I've developed in the course of knowing

you

Loving you long before you loved me

Evolution taught me the detriments of one-sided emo-

tion

Feelings that aren't mutual erode relationships like

moving waters

So I suppressed mine

Hid my smile from you

Well, tried as best I could

Because instead of disappearing, my smile just

Gravitated

Flowed to whichever side you were farthest from

And everyone saw it

But you

I made sure of that

Kept you to one side of me

Distanced

And smiled like a fool on the other side

Not so much for you

But for my own sanity's sake

My own protection

Crooked, huh?

But it's nature

Unnatural human nature

"Fixate"

She writes him poems on her wall with burnt match

sticks when she starts to feel real crazy.

She writes him poems not necessarily about love be-

cause she's not sure if she knows that.

She writes him poems on her wall because at any mo-

ment her mind will recreate him.

She writes him so that he will be still; she hopes he won't

run through her thoughts if she writes him on her wall.

She writes him poems on her wall with burnt match

sticks so her words are few.

She writes a large "I" leaves a space then a large "YOU"

with a myriad of verbs in between.

Crave. Smell. Touch. Like. See. Want. Know. Taste.

Hear. Hold. Remember. Sense. Support. Need. Feel.

Match stick breaks but her list endures.

He makes her feel crazy. Like he's too big to fit in her head so she scribbles him on the expanse of her bedroom wall.

One down. Three to go.

"Arousal"

I was fine with your embrace when you pulled me into

your concrete chest

When you were both the rock and the hard place and I

was locked between you

I was fine

I was fine when you were Moses and I was the seas and

you parted my knees, for all of God's chosen to see, and

leisurely laid between

When you rooted yourself as I grew my limbs around

you

I was fine

I was fine when you beckoned me to sink into your lap

and belted both your arms around my waist

When that happened I was fine

I really was fine

But when I felt the vibrations of your voice

Speaking of white people and privilege and prejudice

As they listened within earshot

My face went hot

My stomach did dance

And silk formed between my thighs

You were fine

You were oh so fine

"Fundamental Reading"

Did you get the love letter I wrote you?

It was really sweet, I promise it was

It talked about how you're like that breeze I felt when I

laid outside in the sultry Tennessee heat

that touched me like it was me without even touching me

at all

Just outlined my silhouette as I tried to outline it with

words

But those got lost in translation like ancient papyrus

scrolls and the love letter I wrote to you that you didn't

seem to get

How did you miss it?

It was the one talking about how you were Xango and I

was Obba and we WERE when WERE was still ARE

And the moment I tried to keep you forever, déjà vu was

born

Cosmically premeditated, I swear I've loved you before

And you haven't read it yet?

I've kissed it on your back

Licked it on your neck

Grazed it across your core

Authored it all over you

It really was a nice letter, you know

I'll write it again, in cursive this time

"Firewood"

Looked inside a fire and saw our kind of love

From two descendants of sinews sparked heat that all

could see

Sounds that some could hear

Gold that none could touch

And we danced from the heat of each other

Burned like lust

Burned like envy

Burned like love

In that golden city deep inside the fire

Flicked, cracked, and consumed each other until there

were only remnants

Two tree-born lovers turned one gray mass

Where all was consumed and confused in that fire

Two children of swaying giants

Opted out of a written love memorial and set it aflame

In the most basic, pure, unbridled way

We were that city of gold

And all coveted our flame

All coveted our fire

"Satin"

He could tell I had something "up my sleeve"

I removed my shirt to show him I did not

He thought there was experience under my belt

I bared my waistline and revealed none

"Surely you'll be the death of me" he says

So I part my limbs and give him life

He is never right in his assumptions of me

But, my god, he never feels wrong

"eCourting"

And i hate that i feel like this

like i'm waiting for you

and telling myself not to

That even though i'm not checking my phone

i'm still wondering

And as stubborn as i am

i refuse to look at it

i won't even carry it on me like normal

i'll leave it zipped up in my bag

Because i can't have-

Because i-

Because i can't be weak

or too invested

or care too much

And i'm trying to convince myself

that not knowing if you called

is better than

knowing you didn't

"Chaos"

Chaos looks like the poem I can't write

Because I fall for you

Seasonally

Like changes of weather

Guiiiiilty smiles

You write, you speak me into existence

And I'm alive with you

It's so crazy

You're good

You're too rich

You're too much

And I get sick

Or I am sick

Because my self tells me don't trust the walking dream

Don't give up your special

So I spring a new season

Come the summered eye of the storm

And I fall back into your chaos

Oo we're crazy, we're sick

We only winter each other for the heat

Of our seasons

"Censorship"

~~I run my hand across you~~

~~Until you are laid flat~~

~~Smooth within my palm~~

~~Rest you firmly between my lips~~

~~Pensively~~

~~Thoughtfully~~

~~Because I need you to know you're all that's on my mind~~

~~And when the coolness of my bed sheets are penetrated~~

~~by the intense heat of your first stroke~~

~~I inhale~~

~~Take you all in~~

~~And ride the seconds into minutes~~

~~And minutes into ours~~

REVISED:

I run my hand across the page

Until it is laid flat

Smooth against my palm

Rest the pen upon my lips

Pensively

Thoughtfully

Because I need you to know what's on my mind

And when the coolness of this white sheet is broken by

the heat of a penstroke

I inhale

Take it all in

And write the seconds into minutes

And minutes into hours

"Fasting"

ONE

On day 1

Before sunset

The gravity

Of his absence

Compiled

All the missing days

To follow

Into

One evening

I have a problem

TWO

I asked for a replica

In lieu

Of the original

The sun is still high

I confuse

Him and night

He won't bring the stars

I hope it stays bright

On day 2

THREE

FOUR

FIVE

We fell short

Like empires

And found

SIX

SEVEN

EIGHT

In the wake

Of our crumbling citadel

We are weak for each other

But of

Unbreakable compliment

NINE

and

TEN

Failed days

Of discipline

"Honeymoon"

She loved him and he loved her

But it wasn't enough

He was still explosive

She was still passive

They still sat back to back

On opposite polars of the bed

Not knowing

That it never has been

Or ever will be

Enough

But, oh, how they were in love

"Pedestal"

I told you I didn't want to be this high

I can't move for fear of falling

And if I lose my footing, you'll idly stand by

Because no man ever caught a de-pedestalled woman

"If You Wonder Why I Don't Believe You"

Most can tell them apart you know

The difference between fresh-squeezed and concentrate

Lays in the perfect sweetness of a replica

Like that between a frozen and a fresh-off-the-vine

Resting in the dryness of preservation

Of trying to make something last longer than it should

And the separation between you loving and you loving

me

Hides in the aftertaste of your lips

A Splenda-soaked semblance of 'similar to'

An indiscriminately bitter 'not quite'

"Daft"

I listened to you out of sequence

That's how we got lost, right?

I didn't start from the beginning

You spoke French, I hummed to the tone of your voice

And although we were simultaneous

We weren't together

And it's not that I can't decipher you now

It's just that I never could

But you were so excited that you were visible

That I couldn't help but smile and mimic your cadence

And look directly into your eyes

Not knowing a thing you said

That's how we got here, right?

Disconnectedly close

"Draft"

I thought about telling you. I honestly did. I even para-phrased it before, and attempted to say it.

But I couldn't let myself do that. I couldn't cross that line, wouldn't even step on it. I'm not that type of person. Even as a kid, they said 'step on a crack, break ya mama back' and here she is, 15 years later, back still together. And even though I don't love you like I do my mama, I do love you. I just can't say it. Sometimes I wonder if I'm bad for you. I picture how you would be if you'd never been with me. You're always happy. You're happy with your 'she' who smiles at you and your parents like her and you're happy. And I watch from third's eye view and keep walking along because I know I don't fit in your happiness. Even now, I don't know where I stand with you and I find myself walking in circles. Because I know there has to be one degree out of those 360 that tells me I'm important to you even if the other 359 say I'm not the one. But feet get tired, my love, and one day I'll have to sit down and watch us end. I just don't want to feel that hurt. That's not terrible, is it? And I know there's no one attacking me, but I need to protect myself. Because I'm all I'll have once you're gone.

Truthfully yours...

"May"

I feel like a child

Curled up on this bed

Trying to forget when we lay like children

Together

And when I slept on one side of the bed

Because the other was occupied

Not because it was cold

"Signed, Your Imperfect Verse"

as your imperfect verse

you can take the liberty of

sprawling me across a white sheet

until the ink is depleted

and the world knows our lyric

you can tell them the spring beginning

where flowers and interests bloomed simultaneously

you can tell them the summer day story

of our sunny park walks

and warm night caresses

of the visible advances

and hidden agendas

of the unwritten agreements of secrecy

and the coded messages carefully scribed on my neck

with your tongue

write these things down into literary history

but please

as you are being acclaimed for your grammatical genius

erase how those summer days fell apart in the fall

as the seasonal heat dissipated

and when the critics rave about your poetic prowess

and revel on your every word

please

omit the winter weeks

when writer's block erased us from existence

and placed me on the page of another poet

just let it suffice that for one beautifully flawed moment

in time

I was your IMPERFECT

verse

as you

slantedly

spraaaaawl me

across your page

"8s"

I carry them with me, you see

Carry them right here in my heart

Those Lovers Passed stay with me

Moments un-departed

Lively memories, ghosts if you will

The hair that draped a whole new world

And protected me from the lights

Drifted across my face like a breeze

Melded with my fingers and invited them in

The arms that held the day into nite

Engulfed and enshrouded in two bodies' heat

Cradled me, cradled me rocked me to sounds

Basses and rhythms, squeezed into me

The body that I was draaawn to

65

Fingertip-engraved scriptures I authored

Carnal sacrifices for offer, on her- off her on her offer...

BREATHE

"Disclosure"

He asked her had she ever been in love

And in that time resting between

Question and answer

She saw another's face

Remembered the stillness of her stomach when he was

near

And the unrequited sickness there when he had gone

In the short time between question and answer

She remembered him

And replied "Nah, I imagine not"

"On the Subject of Men"

I test their love by my lips

None of their tastes satiate

But being the gluttonous child that I am

I consume them anyway

Because when you are hungry enough

And your preference absent

You will eat

That which is edible

So it is not that I am not "right" for them

Or too hard to hold

My tongue is just too dry

My teeth too sharp

To not draw blood from their lips

And water my mouth

At the taste of a kill

"RetOld Fables"

On a day overwhelmed with sunlight

In a kingdom like never seen before

She looked out from atop her throne

And doubted herself

Face stolid and unmoved

Heart wretched

She looked at every face that shone towards her

Every mouth that blessed her steps

Every hope that deemed her 'Queen'

And she doubted herself

Was pulled between the possibilities

Either she would be the pride and protection of her own

reflection standing before her

Or she was vain and selfish

In denial about her connectedness to the rays out yonder

So she sat there, confined in that throne

Unsure if what she'd done was right

And she opened her mouth to speak

With the people hanging on her lips

But made no sound of reassurance

Instead taking that moment to dethrone her doubted self

As the kingdom watched in collective agony

On the day the Queen plummeted 200 feet

Down from Glory's tower

"Reincarnate"

I was a flower before

Something beautiful in a field of other beauties

We all grew toward the same sun

Our beauty was synonymous

Then one day I was plucked and

A flower no more

I could fly once

It took me some time but I did it

I spent half of my life on the ground

Until one day my desire for flight melted it all away

Every part of me

Dissolved

Hurt like hell

But from that matter I made wings

And flew

Drunken and carefree

But the transformation took its toll

And one day I could

Fly no more

I was the air once

I carried life to

Every

Living

Thing

Kept the sky and earth from fighting

God moved through me daily

And I was needed

May not have been loved or appreciated

But I was needed

And this was where I stayed

Through every life

For ever more

And I gave myself life

Sunshine

And flight

"Phonics"

When I was young and still in my Creator's eye

Life taught me how to read

Not moms or dads or schoolcrooks

But winds taught me words

Earth and sky were punctuation

Waters blossomed my prose buds

Life taught me how to read life

"Read it backwards", It said

"Order comes from endings"

I read everything

With infinite hindsight

Knew the harsh that would have to be passed through

To get to the happy

And it always made sense from the end

Every heartache and tear, brushfire and cloud

When I was eye

They all wanted to read like me

But now I read like them

If you can even call it such

"Freedom"

They comfortably set their

Chairs against the door

I twist and twist

Damning my wrist

"Through the Needle's Eye"

I tried to see you clearly

Make you out

And I reached for you

While you just sat there

I could have been standing

Oh God don't let me have been groveling

Because my memory fails me

But the things I do remember are clear

I tried to reach for you and you sat there

Picking at the threads that held me together

Then telling me I'd come undone

That crazy people don't get normal things

While you were my normal

You were every normal thing that I needed and reached

for

That I reached and burst my last seam for

I unraveled right there on the floor before you

You sat and watched me, unmoved

And I died at the feet of your normality

"Soulo"

I will put myself on display

For the mastication of the masses

They will either revere or revolt my offering

But I will have given my contribution

My part will be done

I will trace my mistakes in gold

For them to either worship or bury

But whether polished or in dirt they are precious

Whatever their tomb

I will give them lovelifeliberty

And they will eliminate me for it

Because no one wants light in a world of man-made

shade

But I will be the one they hate

Their diamond in the trash

"Almost Haiku"

I know they tell you not to

But stare at the sun

It

    isn't

        yellow

            at

                all

"Tomorrow Came"

I sat there and that sweet ol' Sun

He kissed my forehead

I've been told those kisses are endearing

I stood there and that soft-toned Sky

He velvetted my skin

It seeped through my pores, I swear it did

I closed my eyes

And became the cool breeze that 70s cats salute to

And nothing could be wrong

Because I saw tomorrow come

Just as the prophet Donny said it would

Only for some

"Programming"

They all wipe their faces

My grandmothers & great-greats

They pray with faces meeting palms

Rebirth by their own hands

My great grandmother had the residue of fallen hopes on

her brow

They were not sullied

But they were heavy

And she couldn't breathe

And didn't know that dreams could feel dirty when they

were not yours

So she cleansed her brown in brown

To reset

Six greats ago the mother of my mothers

Heard herself called

By a name other than her own

She wiped the perspiring accusation from forehead to

chin

Again

And again

She washed their sins

I am no different

I palm my prayers

With oil on my face

Dirt in my dreams

I perspire until I am reborn

My mother showed me how

"Close your eyes, baby girl

But only for a second

Then you come back

You always have to come back"

"As A Little Sister"

My sister gives the sloppiest kisses

Precedes them all with licked lips

I wipe my cheek off with my sleeve

She smiles contently at the gesture

My sister gives the oldest kisses

Like memories from an 80-something

Or childhoods spent in backyards

Fighting off her kissing teenaged boys

My sister gives the saddest kisses

They're always few and far between

Like the one she gave when she moved back home

Or the ones I give when I can't stay

My sister gives me moistened kisses

Like the perspiration on my brow

From our first and only fisticuff

When I suckerpunched her and ran away

She licks her lips; I scrunch my face

But extend my cheek regardless

Who could turn their head away

From their first and oldest friend?

(Oldest referring to her age, not the length of our

friendship; her birthday candles started the Great Fire of

'58.)

"For the First Man I Ever Loved"

To the first man I ever loved,

I spent a portion of my youth not understanding. I didn't understand that what the movies showed and books described wasn't always the standard. I didn't understand that love looked differently than a scripted set of actions. I didn't understand that you weren't perfect. And that thing, more than the others, I held against you. I wasn't old enough to know I had no right to fault you for your humanity. I wasn't mature enough to know that you did the best you could in your own right.

For that, I am sorry.

It took me until my 25th year of observing to realize that everything I pride myself on is because of you. I learned the strength of being vulnerable. I mastered the disciplined business of laughter. I extended my own branch-

es of love. And I knew myself through you. I know my-

self because of you. You may be the Sun, and I the air,

but I carry your heat. I lift up your rays.

Always with love...

"Soul Food"

Outside of this kitchen

Their cold & battered flesh

Seek out for my eyes

To bring them warmth

Life

I got a pot of greens on my stove

And a wooden spoon that never forgets

My grandsons and granddaughters- Thank God &

Amen

- Were baptized in pot liquor

Wiped clean with manna

I got sanity in this succotash

Respect in these ribs

Freedom for a weary soul

In these collards & cornbread

Inside of this kitchen

Spirits flicker like a pilot flame

Rekindle, my children

Thank God & Amen

"Notebook"

She wrote the perfect poem once

Not perfect because of its meter or form

But perfect in its account

It took that Tennessee-spring day

With her face to the sky and back on a slab

Sitting next to a committedly brown boy

Who was either a god or a thug

(the difference between the two

Being comfortably miniscule)

Turned that one day

Into all the days

She had captured the wind in her script

Had lain still and listened to the secrets of old

Whispered in a breeze

Took that experience

Those experiences

And made them a poem

Perfect.

Scribbled in the notebook of a god

Or a thug

She decoded the secrets of the wind

And never saw its perfection again

"Night"

I will remember it.

It was water, wind, and fire

Salinity all around

It was common

It was insignificant

It was comfortable

I will remember it

Comforts are not bountiful

In these days

"The Artist"

She has this pet. It could actually be that she is the animal and it owns her, but her pride and sanity are too fragile to consider this. So for now, she has this pet. It was not naturally hers, but she filed its teeth, clipped its claws, and brought it home. It guarded her door by day and curled in her lap at night. It was all she had.

It would walk with her and tell her she was different. Sleep with her and say that there was no one else like her. Sit with her and tell her that no one would ever truly understand her.

There was only her and her darling pet. She gripped it harder, thinking it was keeping her warm. Really it grasped her tighter, siphoning off more and more of her body's heat.

It was a lonely symbiosis. An alienating thing...when

misery becomes your chosen company.

"Tweed"

Here

We hang about

Strange fruit

With stubborn seed

We always bear flowers

We always bear leaves

"Outro"

I'd like to pay them all homage

The words that were never said

They were so beautiful, you see

That they couldn't be heard

Because all the other words would have lessened in value

And with all that pressure

I'm not sure I could have done them justice

My eloquence is limited

And they are beautiful

More so than my thoughts can attest

They are everything that I have ever wanted to say

Everything I never knew I could